OUR GURNEY TOGETHER

How One Idiot Almost

Killed An Entire Nation

During A Pandemic

A Parody Book About A Joke Of A Human Being

OUR GURNEY TOGETHER

By

Dollhands T. Rump

A Note from the Publisher

For an entire year America, and the World, were subject to idiotic and uninformed opinions about a global pandemic. A failed TV Host who, with the support of the uneducated, fake Christians and white supremacists, was able to slither his way to the most powerful position in the world, and when faced with an actual crisis, managed to screw things up in a way never before seen in our history. Millions of Americans ended up on gurneys, fighting for their lives. Hundreds of thousands of them died, needlessly, as this orange pile of fecal matter scared his deplorable cult against masks, vaccinations, and social distancing...all while telling them to inject bleach, stick UV lights up their butts and whatever other random thing he probably saw on YouTube while surfing the internet while on the toilet. This book is a funny and sad look into what happens when the dumbest of us are given a stage. We regret that we played any part in publishing this book. Dollhands T. Rump is probably one of the worst people to ever walk on this earth, but sadly, we're in the money-making business, and as Ghandi, or someone else once said, 'Shit Sells!'

...or maybe it was Shit Smells...? Oh well, anyway, enjoy!

In December of 2021 I, your great leader, Dollhands T. Rump, me, decided to put out a book about my amazing time in office. I don't want to gloat but I was probably more popular than Abraham Lincoln, Justin Bieber and Betsy Ross combined, and believe me, science will someday figure out how to combine those three, Science is amazing. They do great things. I've always said that! But even a weird LincolnBieberBetsy American Patriot Monster would pale in comparison to how great I was. I was really good. You remember.

Anyway, so they wanted me to make a book about the four years I was in office, but really it was more like 20 years, because of all the great things I accomplished. You can't even count them there were so many. Truly. Don't even try! So they wanted me to write a book but I said no. I reminded them that I don't like things like sentences and paragraphs. Words are hard. So instead I had the great idea of a picture book of just the last year. Who doesn't like a good picture book? They were like, um, okay Boss, whatever you want. I like being called 'Boss'. Sometimes I like being called 'Your Majesty'. Since my time in office I enjoy 'Mr. President', but other people are called that too, and I don't like that, so I'll probably go back to 'Your Majesty' or something like that.

So here it is. A collection of stuff that happened. Then I had another great idea, but really, all my ideas are great. I have the best ideas. But this idea was extra great when I said that I should get to write words next to the pictures. I'll use my Sharpie! I'll write stuff I remember, my thoughts and whatever spills out of my amazing brain. Very exciting, believe me. So here we are. Some photographs with my genius thoughts and probably some other words, who knows, I won't read them. If you think you see any mistakes, spelling and such, it's not a mistake, I just created a new word. You're welcome! I hope you like it and I hope you buy two copies, because I'm still mad they made me give back all that money I stole from some of you on my campaign website, and I want it back. It's mine. All the money is mine! I love you all.

- Dollhands T. Rump (aka Your Majesty)

The Dollhands Administration disbands the White House pandemic response team. They also cut funding to the CDC, by up to 80%, forcing the CDC to cancel its efforts to help countries prevent infectious-disease threats. One of those countries was China.

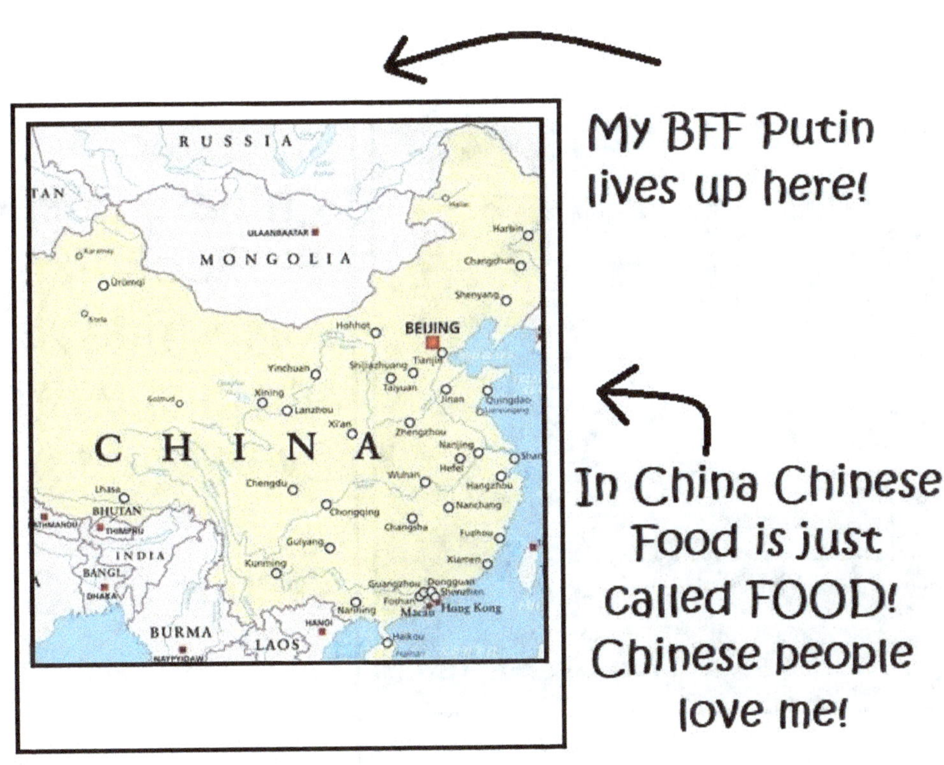

December 2020

Chinese hospitals are seeing patients arriving with "pneumonia-like symptoms."

Chinese hospitals
look like
something you'd
see in the Bronx.
Everyone says so.

Step it up, China!

January 20, 2021

The first confirmed coronavirus case is reported in the United States.

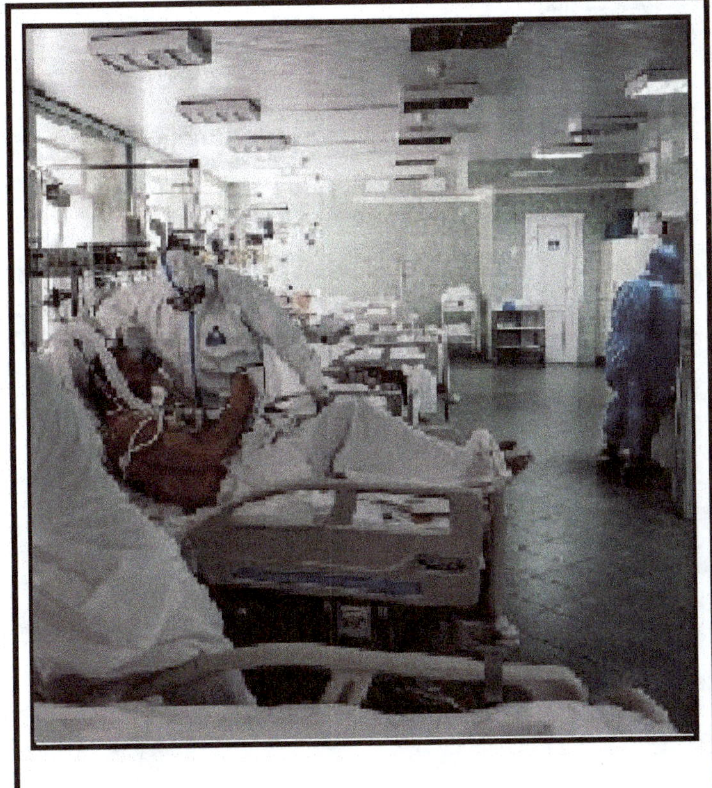

January 22, 2020

"We have it totally under control. It's one person coming in from China. It's going to be just fine." - Dollhands

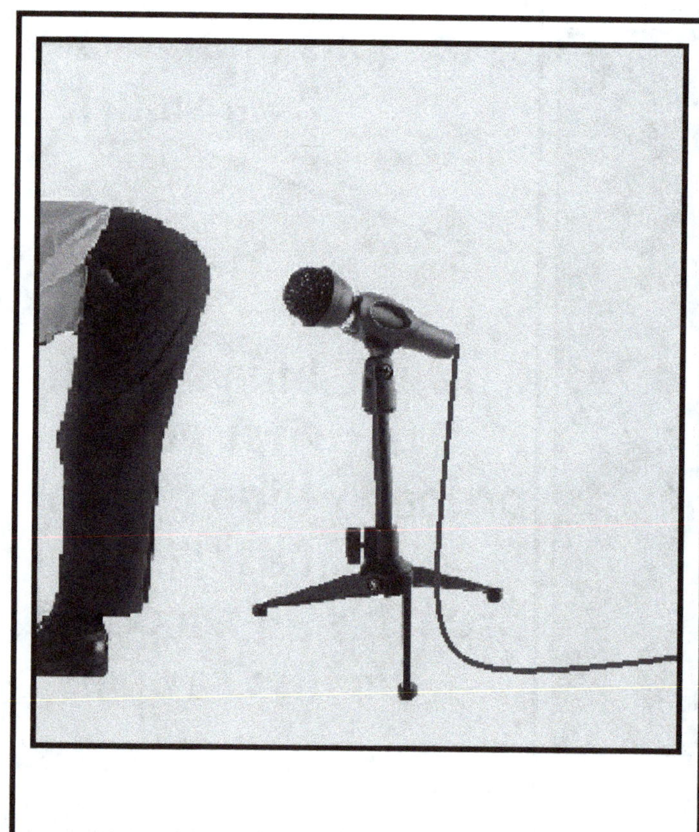

This photo confuses me. Why is there a microphone by my ass? Can people talk out of their butts? Really Confused! I do have nice pants though. Some people say I have the best pants ever! Truth!

January 24, 2020

Dollhands praises China's handling of the coronavirus: "China has been working very hard to contain the Coronavirus. The United States greatly appreciates their efforts and transparency. It will all work out well. In particular, on behalf of the American People, I want to thank President Xi!"

They say I complimented the President of China.
Fake News! He sent us the China Virus! They showed me a fake video of me saying it. Wasn't me! You can't prove it was me! Look at that guy. I don't even know what skin color he is! It was probably the last President! Lies!

February 2, 2020

"We pretty much shut it down coming in from China." - Dollhands

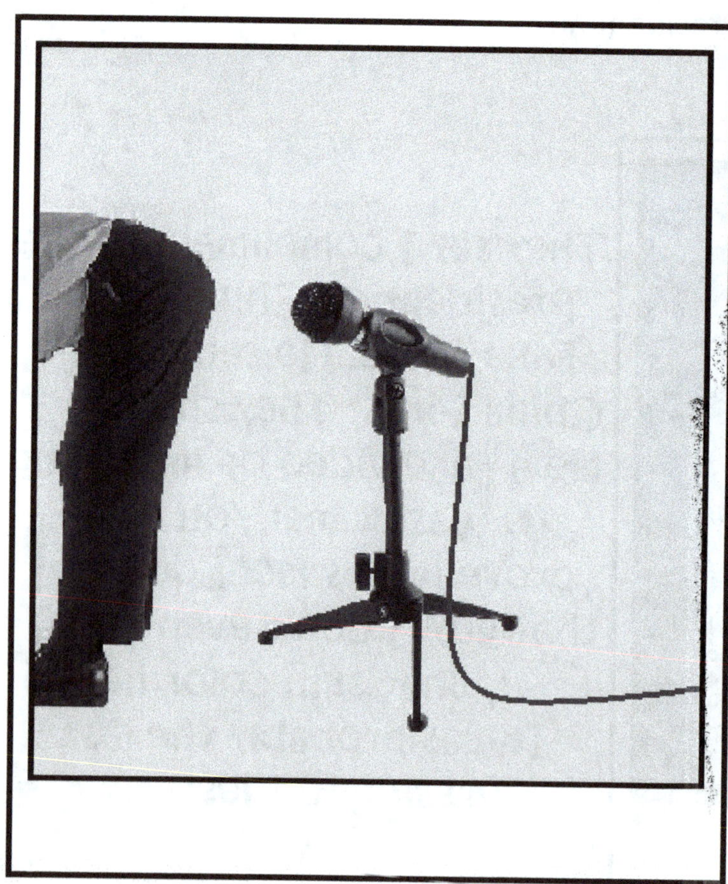

What the hell is with this photo? What does it mean? Is this some stupid 'woke' culture thing? Lame!

"It goes through air, Bob. That's always tougher than the touch. You just breathe the air and that's how it's passed. And, so that's a very tricky one. It's also more deadly than your, you know, your, even your strenuous flus. This is more deadly. This is 5, you know, this is 5% versus 1% and less than 1%. You know, so, this is deadly stuff." — Interview with Woodward, not released until September 2020.

Doesn't my hair look great? They say I have the best hair of any President, ever!

Woodward really screwed me. He asked questions and I answered them. He said he was writing a book but I thought he was lying. Who actually writes their own books??? How was I supposed to know he recorded me saying I lied? I was doing what was best for America! They can't handle the truth! He's just more Fake News!

Feb. 10, 2020

"Now, the virus that we're talking about having to do, you know, a lot of people think that goes away in April with the heat, as the heat comes in. Typically, that will go away in April. We're in great shape though. We have 12 cases, 11 cases, and many of them are in good shape now." — Dollhands

This picture again? It doesn't make sense. It only shows up when I say things that are based on facts...which is always! Whatever. I don't care. I'm going to draw a fart coming out of it. Farts are funny. My kids love to fart. Especially the female one. She has a great sense of humor. That's why she married that pale guy that looks like a mannequin. We all got a good laugh at that! Toot toot!

February 14, 2020

"There's a theory that, in April, when it gets warm — historically, that has been able to kill the virus. So we don't know yet; we're not sure yet. But that's around the corner." — Dollhands

I could have been a scientist. I was super smart in school. I look good in science jackets. Eric and I played with science stuff once. I was the smarter one! He kept lighting his hair on fire. Real scientists tell me I would have been the best scientist. It's true! I could probably invent a cure for cancer if I wanted to. Or maybe make a worse cancer. I chose to make America great instead! Good for America! Bad for cancer!

February 24, 2020

"The Coronavirus is very much under control in the USA. We are in contact with everyone and all relevant countries. CDC & World Health have been working hard and very smart. Stock Market starting to look very good to me!"

— Dollhands in a tweet

Oh! This is one of my favorite photos! The important things I tweeted out that billions and billions of people would read and agree with. Definitely billions! I was the President that tweeted the most in history! They'll probably want to make gold statues of my thumbs some day!

February 25, 2020

"CDC and my Administration are doing a GREAT job of handling Coronavirus."

"I think that's a problem that's going to go away. They have studied it. They know very much. In fact, we're very close to a vaccine."   - Dollhands

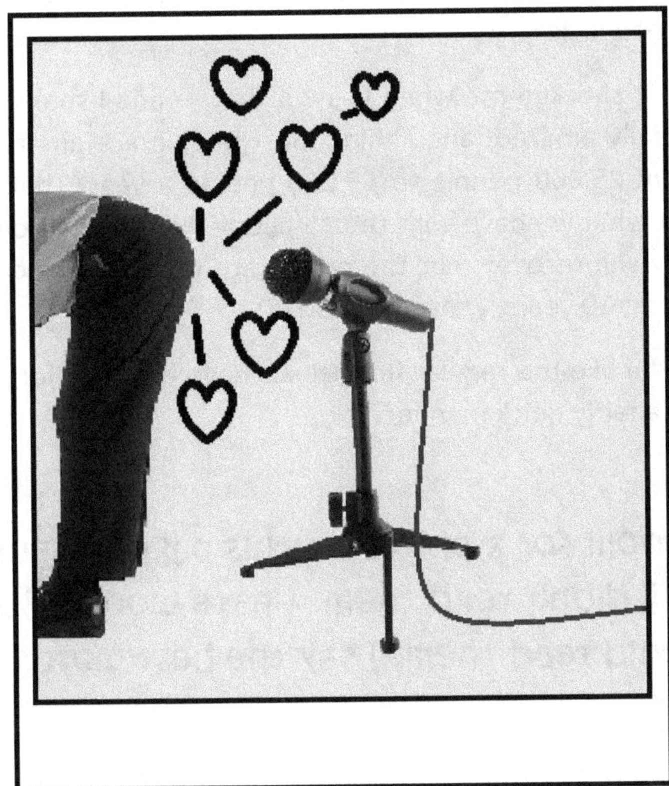

This stupid photo again? Look! I drew hearts coming out of my butt! That's how much I love all my followers. Even my butt loves you! MAGA!

February 26, 2020

"The 15 (cases in the US) within a couple of days is going to be down to close to zero."

"Well, we're testing everybody that we need to test. And we're finding very little problem. Very little problem."

"This is a flu. This is like a flu."

"So we're at the low level. As they get better, we take them off the list, so that we're going to be pretty soon at only five people. And we could be at just one or two people over the next short period of time. So we've had very good luck."

"I want you to understand something that shocked me when I saw it that — and I spoke with Dr. [Anthony] Fauci on this, and I was really amazed, and I think most people are amazed to hear it: The flu, in our country, kills from 25,000 people to 69,000 people a year. That was shocking to me. And, so far, if you look at what we have with the 15 people and their recovery, one is — one is pretty sick but hopefully will recover, but the others are in great shape. But think of that: 25,000 to 69,000. Over the last 10 years, we've lost 360,000."

"But that's a little bit like the flu. It's a little like the regular flu that we have flu shots for. And we'll essentially have a flu shot for this in a fairly quick manner."

--- They tell me there wasn't room for a photo on this page because of all the great words I make. I didn't read them. I hate words. But I probably said them so you should read them. I say the best words. Enjoy! You're welcome!

"It's going to disappear. One day, it's like a miracle, it will disappear."

I've never understood why people got so mad when I said that someday the China Virus would disappear? I didn't say it was going to happen soon, or even years from now, it could take 40 years, but everything disappears. The dinosaurs disappeared. Most legal charges against me disappear. I haven't seen my mushroom penis in over ten years, I'm assuming that disappeared. Calm down. People get so worked up over things I barely said!

February 28, 2020

"We're ordering a lot of supplies. We're ordering a lot of, uh, elements that frankly we wouldn't be ordering unless it was something like this. But we're ordering a lot of different elements of medical."

"So a number that nobody heard of that I heard of recently, and I was shocked to hear it, 35,000 people on average die each year from the flu. Did anyone know that?

"Now the Democrats are politicizing the coronavirus, you know that, right? Coronavirus, they're politicizing it. We did one of the great jobs. You say, 'How's Dollhands doing?' They go, 'Oh, not good, not good.' They have no clue. They don't have any clue.

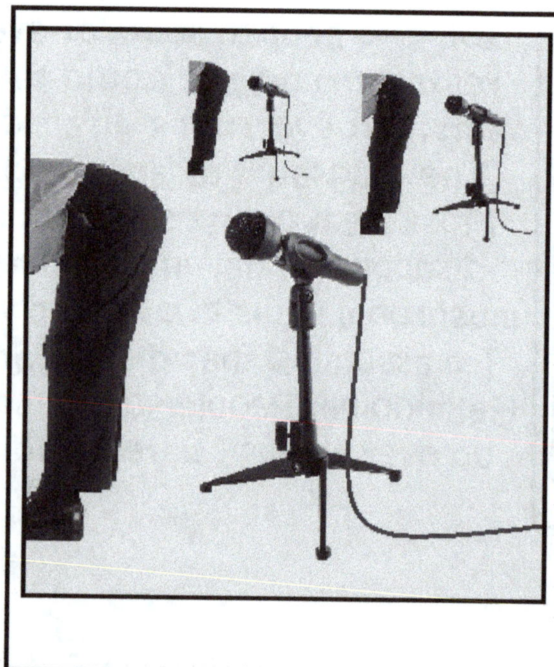

March 1, 2020

Officials warn Rump that the federal response is "NOT fast enough" and that a "very serious public health emergency" was looming. -The Washington Post

This is my favorite photo of me. I think it shows my athleticism. And it also shows how I'm the best golfer. In fact I'm amazing! I win every game! Ask my employees who play against me. I enjoy playing during a pandemic, the course was empty of all those old guys, apparently covid is dangerous for old people. But they'll be fine. I'll save America!

March 2, 2020

"Do you think holding rallies is safe for public health?" — Reporters

"I think it's very safe," - Dollhands

I have the best rallies! Great Americans come to see me and just be near me. I get it. I like being near me too! They love when I hug the flag. I love hugging the flag. It's like hugging my wife, because it doesn't hug back. But I know it loves me!!! I love hugging all beautiful women! Women love when I hug them. My daughter loves it too. Ivanka is a great hugger. People say it's weird how much I like to hug and kiss my daughter. It's not weird. It's a father's love. But like I said when she was younger, if she wasn't my daughter I would probably be dating her. Nothing wrong with saying that. It was a compliment!

March 4, 2020

"If we have thousands or hundreds of thousands of people that get better just by, you know, sitting around and even going to work, some of them go to work, but they get better. Now, and this is just my hunch, and, but based on a lot of conversations with a lot of people that do this. Because a lot people will have this and it's very mild." - Dollhands

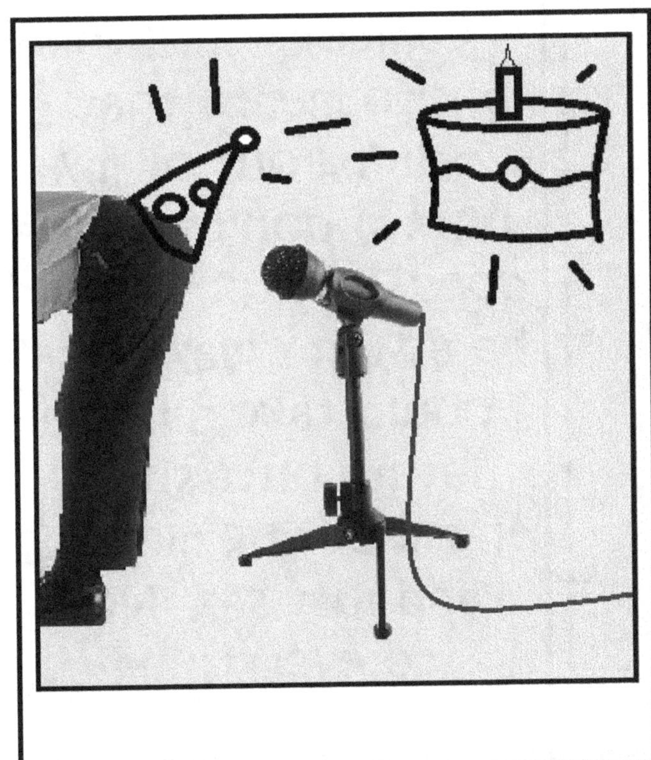

This photo has come up so often I'm giving it a Birthday Party! Look at the butt hat! Ha ha! Happy Birthday, my Ass!

March 6, 2020

"I like this stuff. I really get it. People are surprised that I understand it. Every one of these doctors said, 'How do you know so much about this?' Maybe I have a natural ability. Maybe I should have done that instead of running for president." - Dollhands

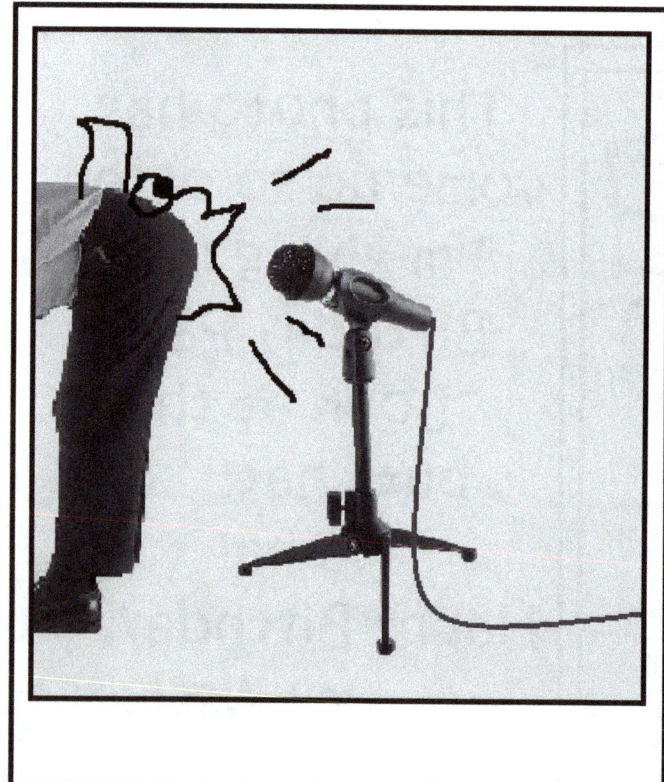

Someone said this photo means that I'm talking out of my butt. I don't think it does. But that would be a funny way to talk! I could take a nap and let my butt sit in those boring meetings and just say "NO!" to everything!

March 8, 2020

"We have a perfectly coordinated and fine-tuned plan at the White House for our attack on CoronaVirus." - Dollhands

My nose looks weird. Must be the lighting.

I'm so proud how the White House worked like a well-oiled machine under my leadership. We nailed it! Experts say there has never been a better running White House. They'll probably write manuals about it so other Presidents can learn from it. You're welcome, America!

March 9, 2020

"So last year 37,000 Americans died from the common Flu. It averages between 27,000 and 70,000 per year. Nothing is shut down, life & the economy go on. At this moment there are 546 confirmed cases of CoronaVirus, with 22 deaths. Think about that!" — Dollhands Tweeting

They tell me my tweets are archived forever. Of course they are! I make the best words. I even invented some words. Like Covfefe! You're welcome!

"And we're prepared, and we're doing a great job with it. And it will go away. Just stay calm. It will go away." — Dollhands to some of his Enablers in Congress

I gave the best speeches to my worshipers in Congress. I kept them in line. They loved me so much. They still do! I'm the best thing to happen to the Party since Lincoln. Probably Better!

March 11, 2020

"It goes away. It's going away. We want it to go away with very, very few deaths." – Dollhands

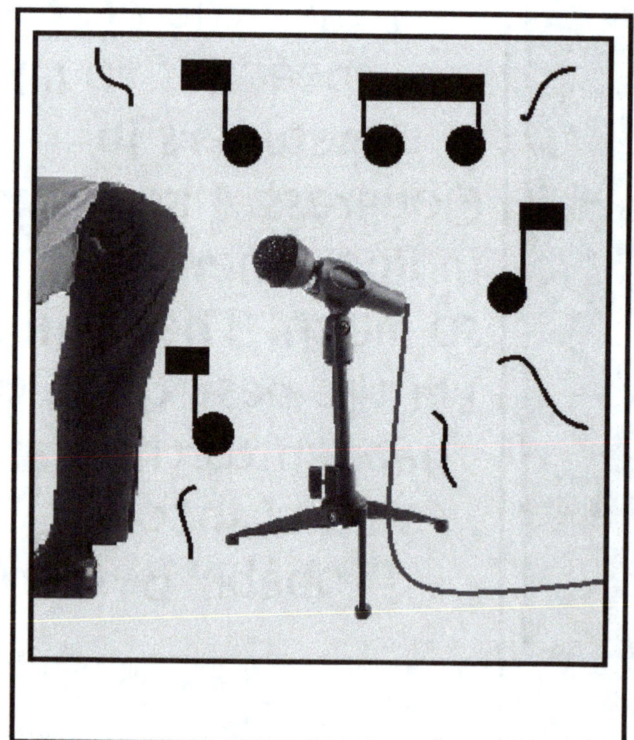

Now my butt is singing something patriotic. Even my butt loves America!

March 13, 2020

The Atlantic reports that 14,000 tests have been administered since the White House knew of this virus, they had promised that by this time we would have had 1.5 million tests done.

"I don't take responsibility at all." - Dollhands

The Fake Media always cried when I told the truth. They hate the truth! But real Americans always were impressed and said to me, "Mr. President, keep telling it like it is, that's why we love you!"

I'm not sure why my head looks like it? It looks like a little mushroom. Weird.

March 15, 2020

"This is a very contagious...this is a very contagious virus. It's incredible. But it's something that we have tremendous control over." — Dollands

I don't know who that French guy is, but I'll tell you this, they LOVED me in France! Loved Me! They couldn't get enough of me. They would tell me "We wish you were our President!" Truth! They wanted to make me a Knight. A French Knight, if that's a thing, I'm pretty sure it is.

March 17, 2020

"I've always known this is a... this is a real... this is a pandemic. I've felt it was a pandemic long before it was called a pandemic."

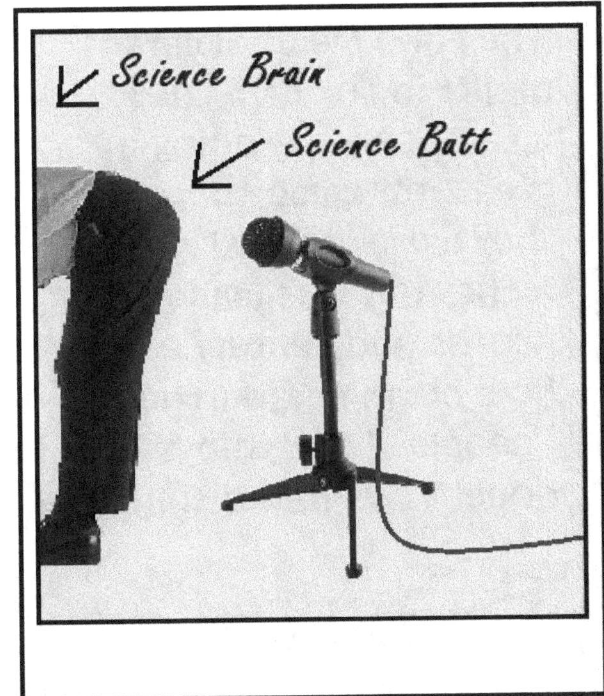

I would have been the best scientist. I have a science brain. Scientists come up to me all the time and say 'Mr. President, we wish you would have become a scientists, we really need you!' And I shrug and tell them that I love science. Love it. I probably love it more than anyone, ever.

But I was needed to save America. I tell them that. And they understand. But they're sad.

Reporter: What do you say to Americans who are watching you right now that are scared?

Dollhands: I say that you're a terrible reporter, that's what I say. I think it's a very nasty question and I think it's a bad signal that you're putting out to the American people.

The Fake News always had it in for me. They hated how easy doing a great job came to me. They were jealous! All they did was make words and sentences, how boring. Sad little people. I got things done! They hated that!

←—LIES!!!

March 22, 2020

"WE CANNOT LET THE CURE BE WORSE THAN THE PROBLEM ITSELF."

The English love me! They say I remind them of one of their Kings. I forget which one. I think he had a bunch of wives just like me! When I visit them hold up signs that say things like 'knob' and 'minge', I assume these are compliments. Too bad they don't speak American, but I understand them. I'm pretty much bilingual.

March 23, 2020

"People get tremendous anxiety and depression, and you have suicides over things like this when you have terrible economies. You have death. Probably and, I mean, definitely, would be in far greater numbers than the numbers that we're talking about with regard to the virus." — Dollhands

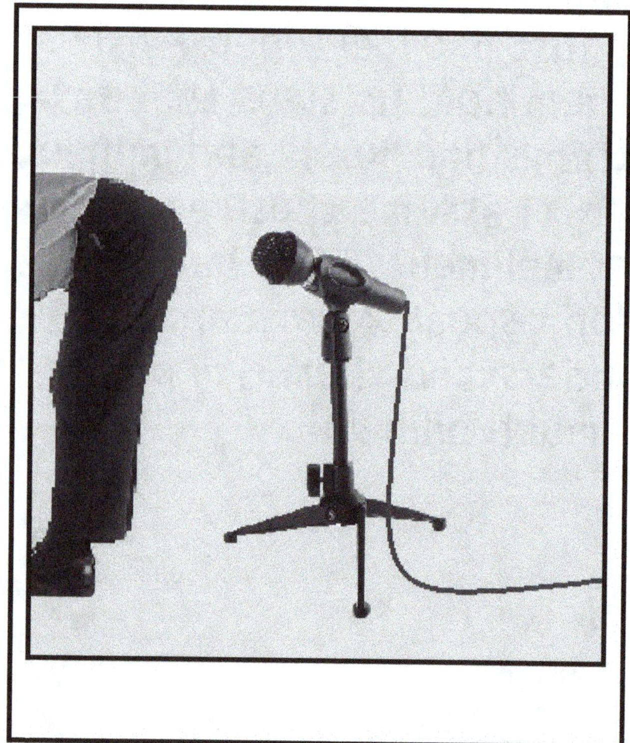

I always have the best words. When they build a monument to me they're going to have a hard time deciding which of my words to use. They'll probably have to build the biggest monument ever! One you can see from space! Maybe they can just carve my speeches into the amazing wall I built between America and Mexico.
Great Idea!

March 29, 2020

Covid Deaths in United States: 780

It was the first time I've been able to play golf since the China Virus came to America. I know during my campaign I said I wouldn't have time to play golf, like that Obummer guy, but it turns out the job of President isn't very hard. I tweet on the toilet, watch six hours of news, sign some things then go to bed. Easy. A dummy could do what I do!

March 26, 2020

The United States becomes the country with the most confirmed coronavirus cases.

"I don't believe you need 40,000 or 30,000 ventilators. You go into major hospitals sometimes, and they'll have two ventilators. And now all of a sudden they're saying, 'Can we order 30,000 ventilators?'"

Lies! All lies! All I was saying is that when the China Virus came the Democrats tried to create a panic and the Doctors and Hospitals were in on it and the panic was a GIANT HOAX and it isn't any worse than the flu. Why can't these hospitals share ventilators? Sounds fishy to me and the Fake News won't investigate all these supposed deaths! Hoax!

March 27, 2020

"We're doing a great job for the state of Washington and I think the Governor...he's constantly chirping and I guess complaining would be a nice way of saying it. I want them to be appreciative. We've done a great job!" – President Rump

That Obummer guy always said he was 'a President for all States,' red or blue, but that's dumb. I'm not helping those States that voted against me. They didn't want to make America great, why should I? Too bad. I think that's what Jesus would have wanted. I'm fairly certain it's in the Bible. I know the whole Bible. I'm probably the best Christian Alive! Truth!

← Not true! I'm 6'3

March 29, 2020

"Unfortunately the enemy is death. It's death. A lot of people are dying. So it's very unpleasant." – Dollhands

President tries to comfort a Nation with random words he just says...

False! So many Americans have told me, "Mr. President, the words you shared are what kept us going." Wise and comforting, they call me, wise and comforting. It's true! I hear important people, very important people, they wanted to start calling me The Comforter in Chief, but I said no, we need to focus on the China Virus first, we can give me names and awards later. They were like okay, we understand, wise one.

March 31, 2020

"I mean, I've had many friends, business people, people with great, actually, common sense, they said, 'Why don't we ride it out?' A lot of people have said, a lot of people have thought about it, 'Ride it out, don't do anything, just ride it out, and think of it as the flu.' But it's not the flu." — Dollhands

This wasn't a lie. Good people with some of the best brains, the HUGEST brains, they told me to just ignore the China Virus and keep making America great...but I told them no, my job is to keep America safe too, and they were like, you're right, sir, you're right as always. I'm probably the safest President we've ever had. I'll probably win a Nobel Peace Prize. A real one. Not like that other guy got.

GREAT MOMENTS IN THE WHITE HOUSE

I was so proud when those big, strong athletes came to visit me at the White House. I know that when I have to visit people I hate when they serve me food I don't like. You don't know how many times I've wanted to tell the President of Japan to just burn me a steak, no one wants to eat octopus! So like the greatest host I served them food that I know a college athlete loves, pizza and hamburgers. They loved it. One even told me that this was possibly the best meal he ever had! Must be something special about eating a Big Mac in the White House with your favorite President.

April 1, 2020

"Because remember, after a month or so … I think once this passes, we're not going to have to be, hopefully, worried too much about the virus." – Dollhands

Local idiot? I'm not local. I'm the damn President of the Free World. I'm a Free World Idiot! And I never said it would be gone in a month. Maybe a few weeks. Maybe a few months. It didn't feel like it would last long, I could tell, just like with my marriages. Sun kills germs! Truth! That's why we don't have the flu in the Summer. It's like microwaving a burrito to kill off the germs! Science!

April 2, 2020

"Massive amounts of medical supplies are being delivered directly to states. Some have insatiable appetites & are never satisfied. The complainers should have been stocked up and ready long before this crisis hit. The Federal Government is merely a back-up for state governments. They have to treat us well, also. They can't say, 'Oh, gee, we should get this, we should get that."

This picture confuses me. Why are they zoomed in on my head? They should have had me take the picture. I take the best pictures. Many picture experts, the best experts, they've told me that I have a perfect eye for pictures and would have been a famous photographer. This is a bad picture. And the arrows don't make sense. Why is there a hole at the top of my head?

April 3, 2020

"So it's voluntary; you don't have to do it. But this is voluntary. I don't think I'm going to be doing it. You can do it. You don't have to do it. I'm choosing not to do it, but some people may want to do it, and that's okay. It's only a recommendation. It's voluntary. I just don't want to be sitting in the Oval Office behind that beautiful Resolute desk, the great resolute desk, wearing a face mask as I greet presidents, prime ministers, dictators, kings, queens, I don't know, somehow I don't see it for myself. I just don't. Maybe I'll change my mind."

Not a big fan of the mask. Sorry. They don't fit right. As you can see, during my 'Executive Time' the mask would always make it hard for me to send my messages to the great Americans who follow my words every day. Masks are like underwear, wear it if you want to, but don't force the rest of us to live so contricted! Free the face! MAGA!

April 6, 2020

U.S. death toll passes 10,000

Look at that form! Great golfers have told me, they were some of the best, they told me I could have been the next Tiger Woods if I had focused on golf instead of real estate. Tiger Woods! That's what they said. I can't argue. I never lose. Oh, and ten thousand dead Americans is awful, just awful. That's all I think about when I'm golfing. Great follow through, right?

April 7, 2020

"You are not going to die from this pill...I really think it's a great thing to try."

- Dollhands promoting Hydroxychloroquine

April 11, 2020

U.S. death toll passes 20,000

I never played golf in a cemetery! Not that it wouldn't be fun. Headstones would be great traps to try and avoid. Anyway, none of my golf courses have cemeteries. They may have been built on old Indian Graveyards, but that's different, no one can see them!

April 15, 2020

U.S. death toll passes 30,000

April 20, 2020

U.S. death toll passes 40,000

April 22, 2020

"So, supposing we hit the body with a tremendous, whether its ultraviolet or just very powerful light, and I think you said, that hasn't been checked but you're gonna test it. And then I said, supposing it brought the light inside the body, which you can either do either through the skin or some other way..."

April 23, 2020

Over 26 million jobless claims have been filed

I would have had the best job numbers in history if the Democrat China Virus hadn't ruined everything. They just couldn't stand seeing me be successful. Probably the most successful President in history! I was better than Lincoln, because I didn't get shot! I like people who don't get shot!

April 24, 2020

U.S. death toll passes 50,000

"The people that know me and know the history of our Country say that I am the hardest working President in history."

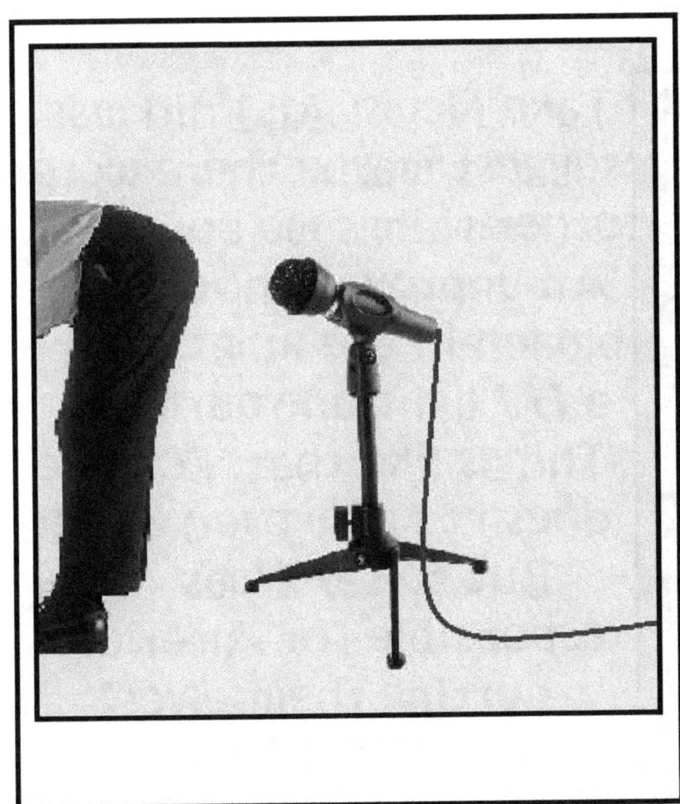

After my first year in office some of the best people, the best people, they said 'Mr. President, you should be on Mount Rushmore', it's true, and I agree. I should be on every mountain, really. I'm that amazing!

April 27, 2020

"I can't imagine why," - Dollhands response to the influx in poison control calls about disinfectant

Fake News! All I did was suggest maybe there were other things we could try. An unproven shot, some bleach in the lungs, maybe a UV light up your butt. Things like that. Science doesn't know everything! But to say I was responsible for Americans hurting themselves, that's Fake News!

April 28, 2020

Confirmed coronavirus cases in the U.S.: 1,000,000

Confirmed coronavirus deaths in the U.S.: 57,000

April 29, 2020

U.S. death toll passes 60,000

"It's gonna go away, this is going to go away." - Dollhands

Wrong! I understand how viruses work. Sometimes I would say things to the scientists, things they hadn't thought of, and they would say to me 'Wow, Mr. President, we never thought of that! Thank you!' All true! I know that a virus can sometimes be stopped by sunlight or bleach. Sometimes they disappear. Poof! Like magic. I think Polio did that. Poof! Polio was gone one day.

April 30, 2020

"But as far as where I'm going in Arizona, I'm going to have to look at the climate. I'd have no problem wearing a mask. I don't know. I'm supposed to make a speech. I just don't know: Should I speak in a mask? You're going to have to tell me if that's politically correct. I don't know. If it is, I'll speak in a mask."

I love Arizona! Great patriots! And scorpions. Big ones! They'll bite your head off! Truth! They also had that great sheriff that made bad guys wear pink underwear. That was funny. And that lady governor. She wasn't much to look at. She looked like a crypt keeper. Maybe she needed to moisturize. But she was good. She yelled at Obummer, that was great!

May 3, 2020

"On Jan. 23, I was told that there could be a virus coming in, but it was of no real import. In other words, it wasn't, oh, we have got to do something, we have got to do something. It was a brief conversation. Also, they only spoke of the Virus in a very non-threatening, or matter of fact, manner. " – Dollhands

See? Even my own staff agrees that I was not informed how bad this virus would be. And I do pay attention in security briefings, even to the blah blah blah. I've told them before, words are boring, if you want me to pay attention draw me a nice pie chart or a graph with squiggly lines. How hard is that? If it's not in a pie chart than it can't be important!

May 5, 2020

U.S. death toll passes 70,000

"You know, the virus will pass. There'll be more death, the virus will pass, with or without a vaccine. And I think we're doing very well on the vaccines but, with or without a vaccine, it's going to pass, and we're going to be back to normal."

May 6, 2020

The Brookings Institution reports that children are experiencing food insecurity to an extent unprecedented in modern times. Republicans block proposals to expand food stamps.

My eyes aren't red! Fake News! Republicans DO care about children. STOP abortion is what I always yell. Sure, we may not care much about kids in poverty, or their education, or their safety during a pandemic, but give us an unborn child and we'll march in the streets to make sure they get out of that belly. Sure, they may die later while in school, but being shot in school is part of their freedom as an American Citizen! The red hats are beautiful! It's all lies about China, only the tags are Made in China.

May 7, 2020

Over 33 million jobless claims have been filed

The beautiful patriots shouted JOBS at my rallies and that's what I gave them. One smart person said I've created more jobs than any President in history. It's probably true. Another smart person, very smart, said I may have created more jobs than every President combined. I don't know. That's what they say. I think we may find out that I created more jobs than there are actual people in the world! MAGA!

May 11, 2020

U.S. death toll passes 80,000

"Coronavirus numbers are looking MUCH better, going down almost everywhere. Big progress being made! We have met the moment and we have prevailed!"

May 14, 2020

"Don't forget, we have more cases than anybody in the world. But why? Because we do more testing, so we have the best testing in the world. It could be that testing is, frankly, overrated. Maybe it is overrated."

Not true! I know how testing works. You have 100 people in an orgy, and one of them has herpes, you don't test the other 99. You'll only find more herpes! No one will want to join. Bad salesmanship! I should know. I'm the best businessman. I even wrote a book about it. Bestseller!

GREAT MOMENTS IN WHITE HOUSE HISTORY

They say you can judge a man by the friends he keeps...

May 16, 2020

"We've done a GREAT job on Covid response, making all Governors look good, some fantastic, and that's okay, but the Lamestream Media doesn't want to go with that narrative, and the Do Nothing Dems talking point is to say only bad about "Rump". I made everybody look good, but me!" - Dollhands

Oh, how lucky you are! Me as a baby. I was the best baby. My mother's housekeeper said I was probably her favorite baby she ever raised. Smartest too! Look at that hair. I came out of the womb with that hair. They said the Doctor told my parents I was going places the moment he looked at me. Those aren't tears. That's Fake News! I never cried.

May 18, 2020

U.S. death toll passes 90,000

May 19, 2020

"When we have a lot of cases, I don't look at that as a bad thing, I look at that as, in a certain respect, as being a good thing. Because it means our testing is much better. I view it as a badge of honor, really, it's a badge of honor."

The Lamestream Media completely misunderstood what I said. The more testing we do the more sick we find, the more we find the more people will die, sure, but it also means the more sick people we find then we're doing AMAZING at the testing. Great testing. How come the Dummycrats can't focus on that? They're always negative. MAGA!

May 25, 2020

"Great reviews on our handling of Covid 19, sometimes referred to as the China Virus. Ventilators, Testing, Medical Supply Distribution, we made a lot of Governors look very good. And got no credit for so doing. Most importantly, we helped a lot of great people!" — Dollhands on the Toilet

Someone once joked that my Presidential Monument will be a giant, stone carving of me sending one of my amazing tweets. I like that idea. I think about it a lot. It can be at the base of the Washington Monument, you know, the one that looks like a giant shaft. I'll be at the bottom of the shaft. It will be beautiful. I deserve to be at the bottom of a great man's shaft.

May 27, 2020

U.S. death toll passes 100,000

May 29, 2020

"We will be today terminating our relationship with the World Health Organization"

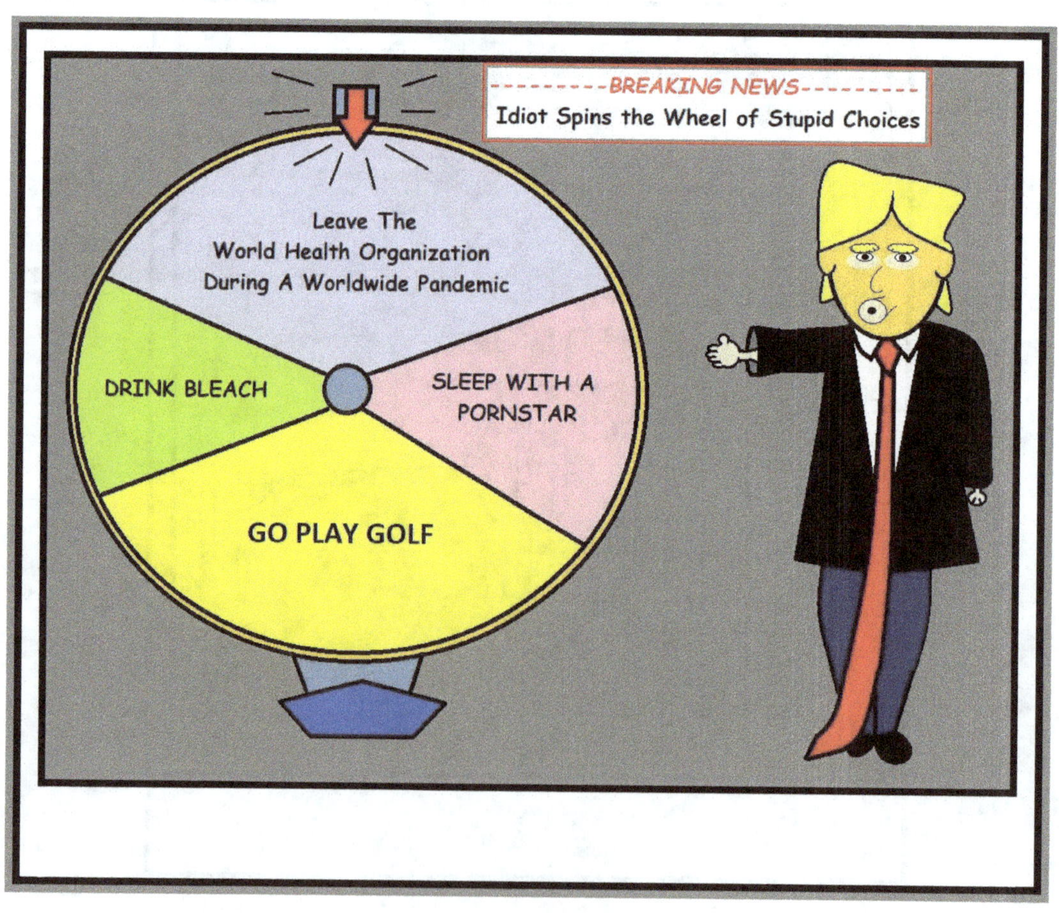

June 6, 20202

"Hopefully George [Floyd] is looking down right now and saying this is a great thing that's happening for our country. This is a great day for him. It's a great day for everybody. This is a great day for everybody. This is a great, great day in terms of equality." - Dollhands

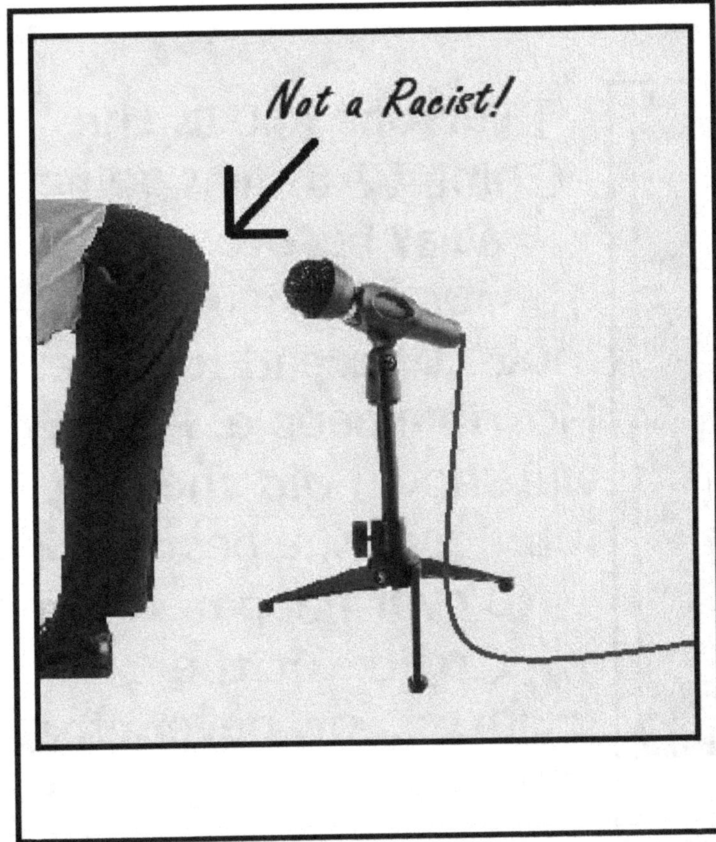

The Lamestream Media said my remark about George Floyd was racist. Bullshit! No one is less racist than me! I'm less racist toward Blacks than actual Blacks. Truth! I have Black friends, I have Black employees. Hell, once I even cheated on my wife with a Black prostitute. Would a racist do that? I don't think so. Idiots!

June 15, 2020

"At some point this stuff goes away and it's going away." - Dollhands

Everyone knows the China Virus was going away before the Democrats figured out how to spread it faster. Horrible people. History will show I did the best job. I was the best thing to ever happen to Covid...or the worst....or, nevermind, you know what I mean!

June 20, 2020

"They call me, they say the job you're doing…here's the bad part, when you test of…when you do testing to that extent, you're going to find more people, you're going to find more cases. So, I said to my people slow the testing down, please. If we didn't do testing, we'd have no cases – Dollhands

It was dumb how many people didn't understand what I was trying to say. Smart people, the smartest, told me I was correct. You do less testing you get less positive results. Simple. Just like I told my policeman friend, if you pull over less swerving vehicles, you have less DUI arrests, then you've fixed drunk driving! Simple! And that's not my hat. Mine doesn't have words on it…and it has eye holes.

June 22, 2020

U.S death toll passes 120,000

June 25, 2020

(The U.S. has 4% of the global population and 25% of deaths)

"Coronavirus deaths are way down. Mortality rate is one of the lowest in the World. The Fake News Media won't tell you that…you're going to have a kid with the sniffles, and they'll say it's coronavirus…whatever you want to call it."

Who is this woman?
Is she an immigrant?
Immigrants love me!
Is she accusing me of
sexual harrassment?
LIES! I would never
sexually harrass her.
She's not my type!
What's behind her?
A dog? Are those
weird trees?

July 1, 2020

"I had a mask on. I sort of liked the way I looked, OK? I thought it was OK. It was a dark black mask, and I thought it looked OK. Looked like the Lone Ranger."

What does cheating on my wives have to do with being a superhero that hangs out with cool Indians? Fake News! Trying to make me look bad. And technically, I cheated on my wives with future wives, so that's not really cheating. I think the Bible says that's okay. Look it up!

July 7, 2020

"I think we are in a good place." - Dollhands

U.S. death toll passes 130,000

July 8, 2020

"In Germany, Denmark, Norway, Sweden, and many other countries, SCHOOLS ARE OPEN WITH NO PROBLEMS. The Dems think it would be bad for them politically if U.S. schools open before the November election, but it is important for the children & families. May cut off funding if not open!"

Democrats don't care about education as much as I do. I'm pretty much the Education President! Education is very important. We didn't focus on Eric's education and look what happened to him. That's one dumbass kid. That's why we named him Eric, after the dog.

July 9, 2020

"They have been wrong about a lot of things, including face masks. Maybe they are wrong, maybe not. But a lot of them said, don't wear a mask, don't wear a mask. And now they are saying, wear a mask."

Masks! Masks! Masks! These idiots don't know what they're doing. The China Virus doesn't care if you're wearing a mask, it only cares about how patriotic you are, or how much Jesus likes you! Truth! That's why I'll never get sick!

July 18, 2020

U.S. death toll passes 140,000

July 20, 2020

"We are united in our effort to defeat the Invisible China Virus, and many people say that it is Patriotic to wear a face mask when you can't socially distance. There is nobody more Patriotic than me, your favorite President!" — The Twit Tweeting

July 21, 2020

"You will never hear this on the Fake News concerning the China Virus, but by comparison to most other countries, who are suffering greatly, we are doing very well and we have done things that few other countries could have done!"

I don't understand why this picture of baby me keeps showing up. I know i'm adorable! I was momma's little mushroom!

July 28, 2020

U.S. death toll passes 150,000

July 29, 2020

"He's (Dr. Fauci) got this high approval rating. So why don't I have a high approval rating with respect and the administration, with respect to the virus?" - Dollhands

I don't know what that guy is yapping about. Too many words! You know I hate words. But it does look like he's wearing one of my MAGA hats...so I like him! He's probably saying I'm his hero. I get that a lot. I'm my hero too!

August 3, 2020

"I think we are doing very well and I think ... as well as any nation,"   "They are dying. That's true. And it is what it is."   "OPEN THE SCHOOLS!!!"   "Right now I think it's under control."   "We've done MUCH better than most other Countries in dealing with the China Virus. Many of these countries are now having a major second wave. The Fake News is working overtime to make the USA (& me) look as bad as possible!"

This is my favorite photo of me. I wanted to make this my Christmas Card for the Fake Media, but my advisors told me it wasn't Presidential, whatever that means. I like that i'm wearing a hat calling them all Dipshits! You can tell it was a message for them, right? Maybe I should have put an 's' at the end of it? Oh well. Still love it. Merry Christmas,
Fake News Dipshits!

August 6, 2020

U.S. death toll passes 160,000

August 7, 2020

Dollhands holds a press briefing inside the Dollhands National Golf Club in New Jersey that was attended by golf club guests, many without face masks or practicing social distancing in violation of state guidelines. When asked "why are you setting such a bad example," Dollhands told the reporter: "You know, you have an exclusion in the law. It says 'peaceful protest' or 'political activity,' right? I'd call it 'peaceful protests' because they heard you were coming up. And they know the news is fake."

The media loves me. They pretend they don't, but those idiots know I make them money! I could call them fake news and they put it all over the airwaves, pretending they're offended, then they come back for more. They're like crackheads looking for their next fix. They'll never be able to stop interviewing me. I'm why they sell newspapers. Truth!

August 11, 2020

"America is winning the war against the virus."

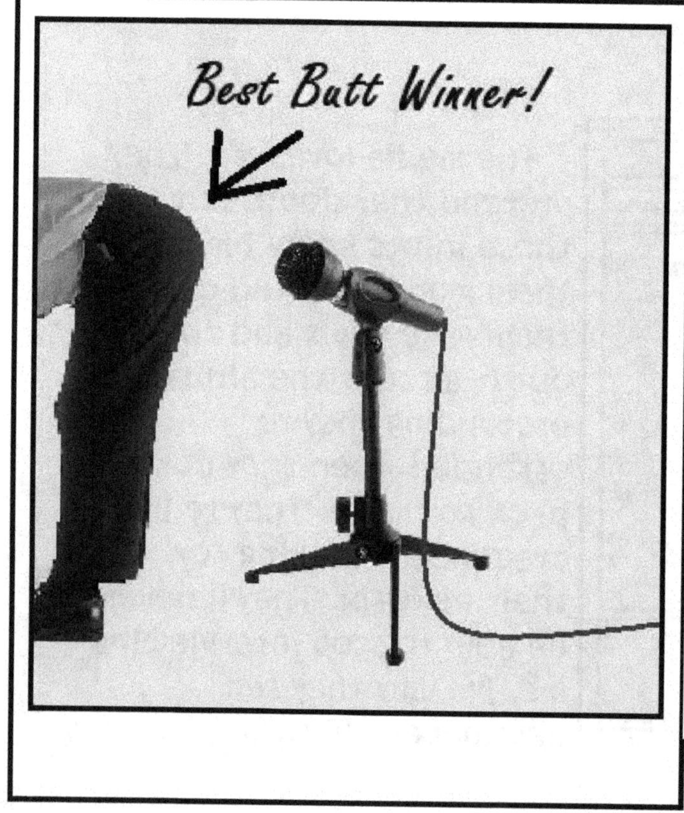

You guys really like my butt, don't you? Every time I say something I swear, there's my butt! That's fine. I was actually voted best butt in my private school. Seriously!

August 16, 2020

U.S. death toll passes 170,000

August 18, 2020

"Shutdowns cause, I think probably, or possibly, much bigger problems than even the virus itself."

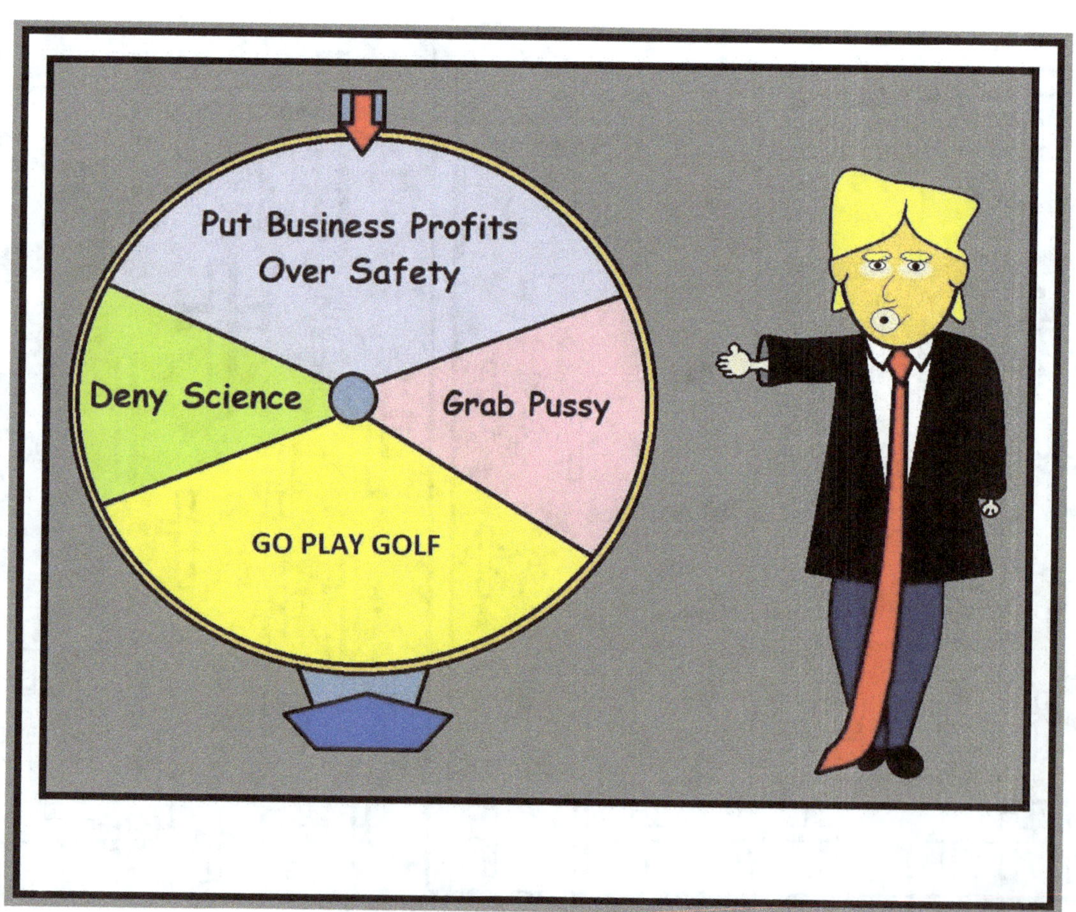

August 19, 2020

"You're killing me! This whole thing is! We've got all the damn cases...I want to do what Mexico does. They don't give you a test till you get to the emergency room and you're vomiting!" – Dollhands yelling at his idiot son-in-law

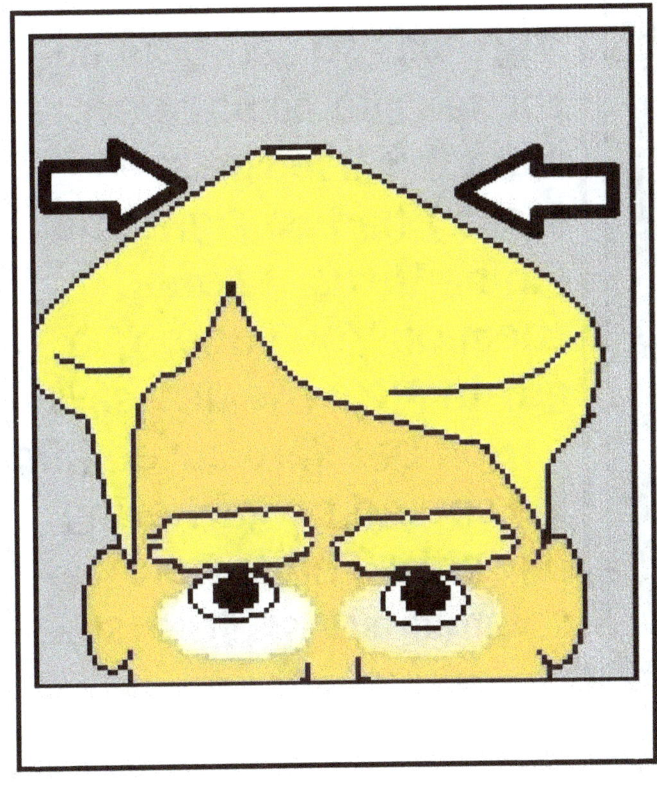

How the hell do people not understand that if you stop tesing then you stop having infections??? Am I the only person alive who understands science? My daughter's idiot husband didn't get it either! He's a moron. He's lucky his father is rich or she never would have looked at him.

August 22, 2020

"Many doctors and studies disagree with this!" – Dollhands tweet-crying that the FDA is revoking hydroxychloroquine and chloroquine for COVID-19 treatment, as they are "unlikely to be effective"

It was so sad how all those fake news doctors wouldn't use the great ideas I had to fight the China Virus. I found them on YouTube. If a guy in New Mexico says eating bat shit cured him we should be gathering bat shit! That's how science works! Idiots!

August 23, 2020

"Today, I'm pleased to make a truly historic announcement in our battle against the China virus that will save countless lives. The FDA has issued an emergency use authorization, and that's such a powerful term: emergency use authorization, for a treatment known as convalescent plasma, it has proven to reduce mortality by 35%." – Dollhands makes false claims, out loud, as usual

Fake News! That wasn't a lie! I was told those facts by an actual doctor. I don't remember who. He had on a white coat. Or a white shirt. He definitely had on glasses. Everyone smart wears glasses, except me, I have perfect eyes. The best eyes around. They say it's from looking directly into the sun. History will show how I saved America...and had amazing eyes!

August 24, 2020

"And when we get rid of this, this virus, which will happen, and it will happen sooner than people think and that's with the vaccines, but even without the vaccines. It's happening."

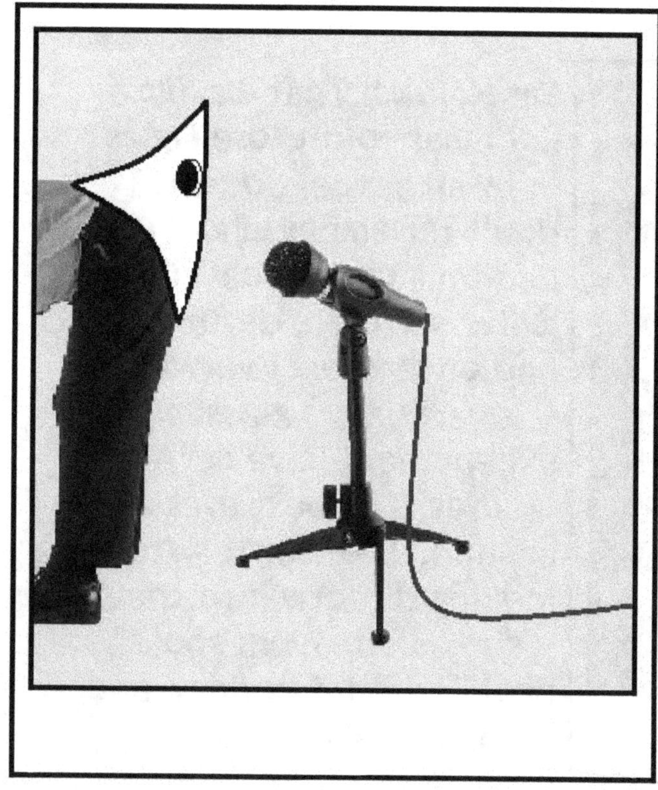

You'll all see. By 2021 this will all just be a bad memory and the China Virus will be gone. I'll be your Hero President for four more years, maybe eight more, and America will become Great the way we were in the 1950's, when everyone knew their place! MAGA!

August 26, 2020

U.S. death toll passes 180,000

August 28, 2020

"I want football back. These are young, strong guys, they're not going to be affected by the virus. If you look at it, it's generally older people, older people that have heart conditions, that have diabetes, that have problems."

September 3, 2020

"I've never seen a man [Biden] that liked a mask more. Look, I'm all for it, but did you ever see a man that likes a mask as much as him? And then he makes a speech and he always has it, not always but a lot of times he has it hanging down because you know what, it gives him a feeling of security. If I were a psychiatrist, right? No, I'd say, I'd say this guy has got some big issues."

All I was saying is that I don't live in fear. If that China Virus came up to me I would just grab it by the pussy and show it who is boss! But not Sleepy Joe! If he had his way we'd all be hiding underground instead of opening up America again! We can't be great in a basement!

"So, on the China virus front, the nations of Europe have experienced a 38% greater excess mortality than the United States. 38% more greater excess mortality than the United States. A lot of you don't want to report that. The job we've done is incredible. We've done a fantastic job on this China virus, the invisible enemy. I get no credit for it." — Dollhands makes claims that were all shown to be FALSE

History will show I was right! History will show that I was a Great President! The same way it shows how Nixon was really a man of honor! Monuments will be built for me. You just wait and see. Believe me!

September 10, 2020

U.S. death toll passes 190,000

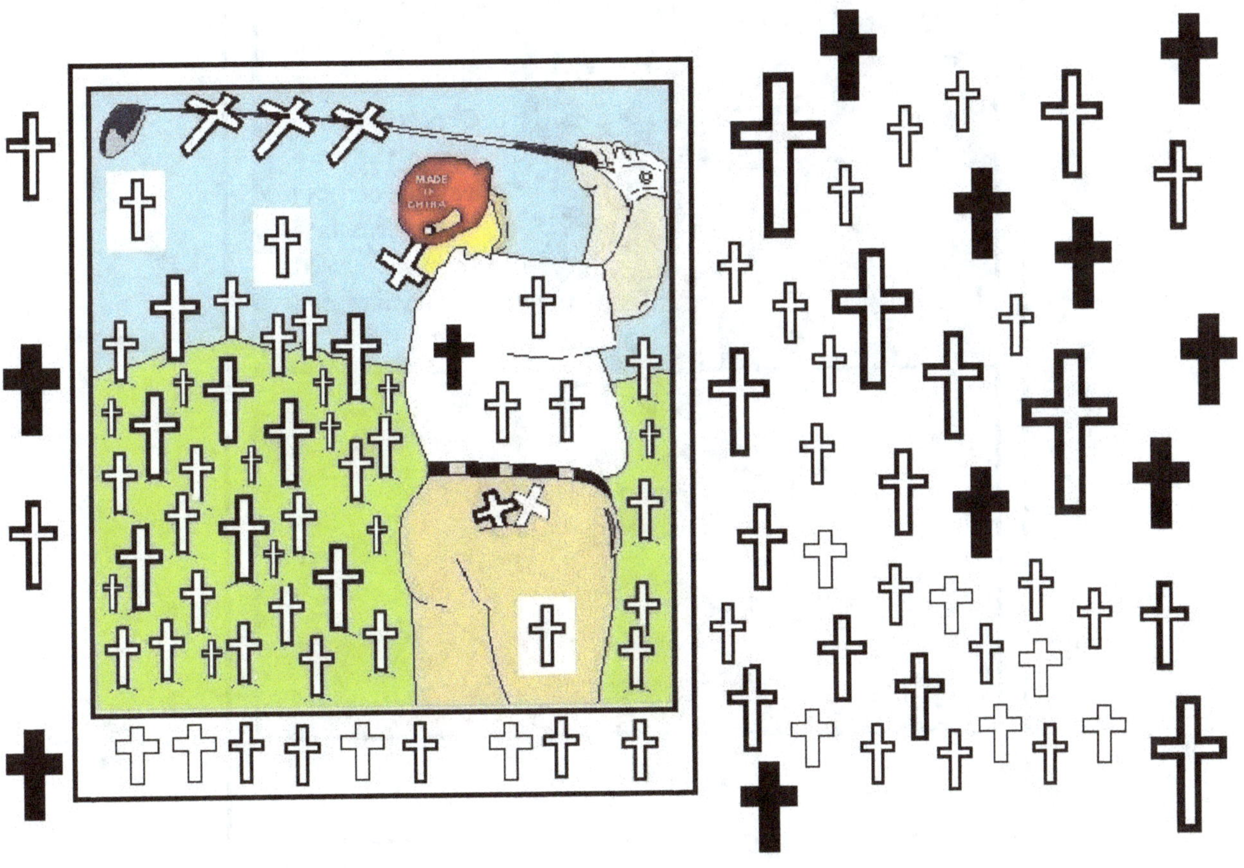

September 14, 2020

Dollhands was asked if he is afraid of Coronavirus risk at his rallies:

"I'm on a stage, it's very far away, so I'm not at all concerned."

September 18, 2020

"You don't have to wear masks at protests. So I said, 'You know, we can't have a rally.' The most we can have is 10 people, but why don't we just call it a protest because this is a protest. It's a protest against stupidity." — Dollhands finding a way to gather thousands of deplorables and spread the virus, just so he can hear people applaud him

September 19, 2020

U.S. death toll passes 200,000

September 21, 2020

"It affects elderly people, elderly people with heart problems, and other problems. If they have other problems, that's what it really affects. That's it. You know, in some states thousands of people, nobody young, below the age of 18, like nobody. They have a strong immune system. Who knows? They look at you, take your hat off to the young because they have a hell of an immune system, but it affects virtually nobody."

September 24, 2020

"The China virus, it's China, some people call it coronavirus. That sounds like a beautiful place in Italy, right? No, it didn't come from Italy. It came from China. But this guy's talking, he'll shut it down. If the scientists say shut it down, he'll shut it down. No, we're not shutting anything down. … My plan will crush the virus and we're doing it. We're rounding the third. We're rounding the turn."

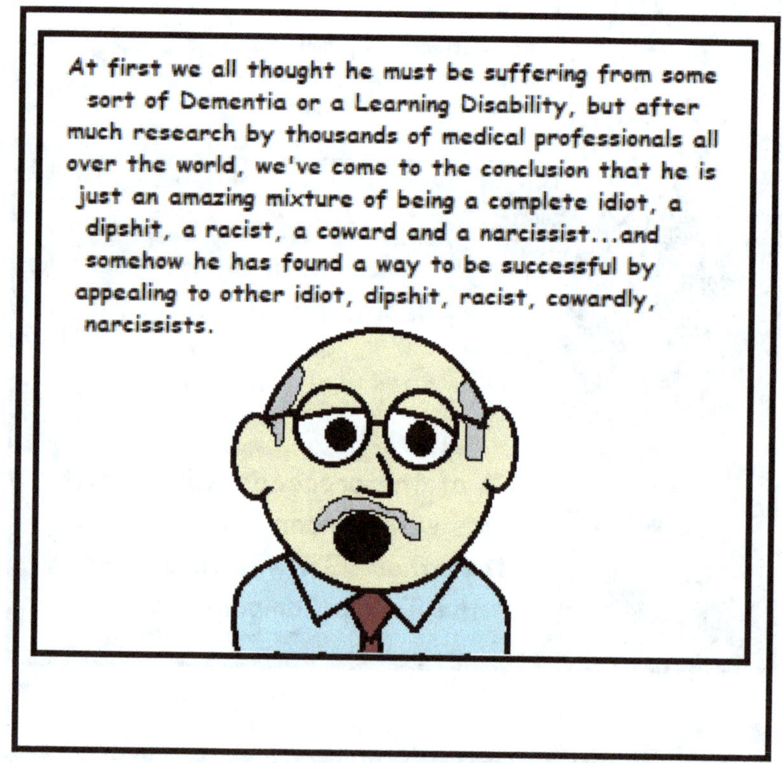

September 29, 2020

Members of Dollhand's family did not wear masks during the debate.

Later we find out that Dollhands had tested positive for Covid days before the debate.

Below is a blank space for you to draw your own picture of what a bunch of asshole dickheads, from all one family, would look like.

October 2, 2020

Dollhands and the shit-personality First Lady test positive for Coronavirus.

Later we find out they had tested positive DAYS EARLIER, but kept it hidden so he could go to the debate. He also attended a meeting with GOLD STAR FAMILIES, most likely infecting them as well...because he Supports our Troops...by killing off their families.

The still infectious, idiot President takes a car ride around the hospital, putting his Secret Service guys at risk, all so he could wave at his deplorable cult and feed his fragile ego.

Look how much they love me! I'm like a hero to them. They were impressed how strong I was after being infected by the China Virus. My American blood was why I am okay. Losers die from this. It only made me stronger! It's like I have a superpower, along with being so smart and so handsome, I'm like AntiChinaVirus Guy! MAGA!

October 5, 2020

U.S. death toll passes 210,000

Dollhands response…"Don't be afraid of Covid."

"Many people every year, sometimes over 100,000, and despite the Vaccine, die from the Flu, Are we going to close down our Country? No, we have learned to live with it, just like we are learning to live with Covid, in most populations far less lethal!!!"

Fake News! These doctors don't know what they're talking about. I could have been a doctor, but I hate wearing white, unless it comes with a matching hood. The Fake News just wants to scare you so they can get their Socialist agenda person elected.

October 12, 2020

"I went through it. Now, they say I'm immune. I can feel—I feel so powerful."

October 18, 2020

"He'll listen to the scientists... If I listened totally to the scientists, we would right now have a country that would be in a massive depression instead — we're like a rocket ship. Take a look at the numbers." – Dollhands T. Rump

The Numbers: U.S. death toll surpasses 220,000

October 19, 2020

"People are saying whatever. Just leave us alone. They're tired of it. People are tired of hearing Fauci and all these idiots. Fauci is a nice guy. He's been here for 500 years. They are getting tired of the pandemic, aren't they? You turn on CNN, that's all they cover. 'Covid, Covid, Pandemic, Covid, Covid.' You know why? They're trying to talk everybody out of voting. People aren't buying it, CNN, you dumb bastards."

WRONG! I've never thrown a tantrum. I said what the American people were thinking. Time to open things up! Only old people are dying. We need sports back. Sports is more popular than old people! Everyone knows that! That's why we spend billions on sports and next to nothing on old people!

October 20, 2020

Politico reports that The White House is considering slashing millions of dollars for coronavirus relief, HIV treatment, screenings for newborns and other programs in Democratic-led cities that President Dollhands has deemed "anarchist jurisdictions," most likely causing hundreds to thousands of unnecessary deaths.

Oct. 24, 2020

"Turn on television: 'covid, covid, covid, covid, covid.' A plane goes down, 500 people dead, they don't talk about it — 'covid, covid, covid, covid,' By the way, on November 4th, you won't hear about it anymore." - Dollhands

I never held up a sign like that! Fake News! All I said was the virus will suddenly disappear if Sleepy Joe wins, but he won't win, we're making America great, who wouldn't vote for that? I also don't have a little peepee. Just ask the prostitutes i've been with. Not the Russian ones. They don't speak English. That's why they misunderstood me when I asked them to get me a drink and they started peeing on the bed. Horrible! What? Never happened! I've never even been to Russia. Lies! Anyway, my penis is huge! Just don't ask my wife. She will lie. She hates how big it is. That's why she won't touch it. It scares her!

October. 26, 2020

"Cases up because we TEST, TEST, TEST. A Fake News Media Conspiracy. Many young people who heal very fast. 99.9%. Corrupt Media conspiracy at all time high. On November 4th, the topic will totally change. VOTE! We have made tremendous progress with the China Virus, but the Fake News refuses to talk about it this close to the Election. COVID, COVID, COVID is being used by them, in total coordination, in order to change our great early election numbers. Should be an election law violation!"

October 30, 2020

"Our doctors get more money if someone dies from Covid, and so when in doubt choose Covid." – Idiot in Chief

November 1, 2020

"Biden wants to LOCKDOWN our Country, maybe for years. Crazy! There will be NO LOCKDOWNS. The great American Comeback is underway!!!" – Dollhands

230,000 Americans have now died of Covid

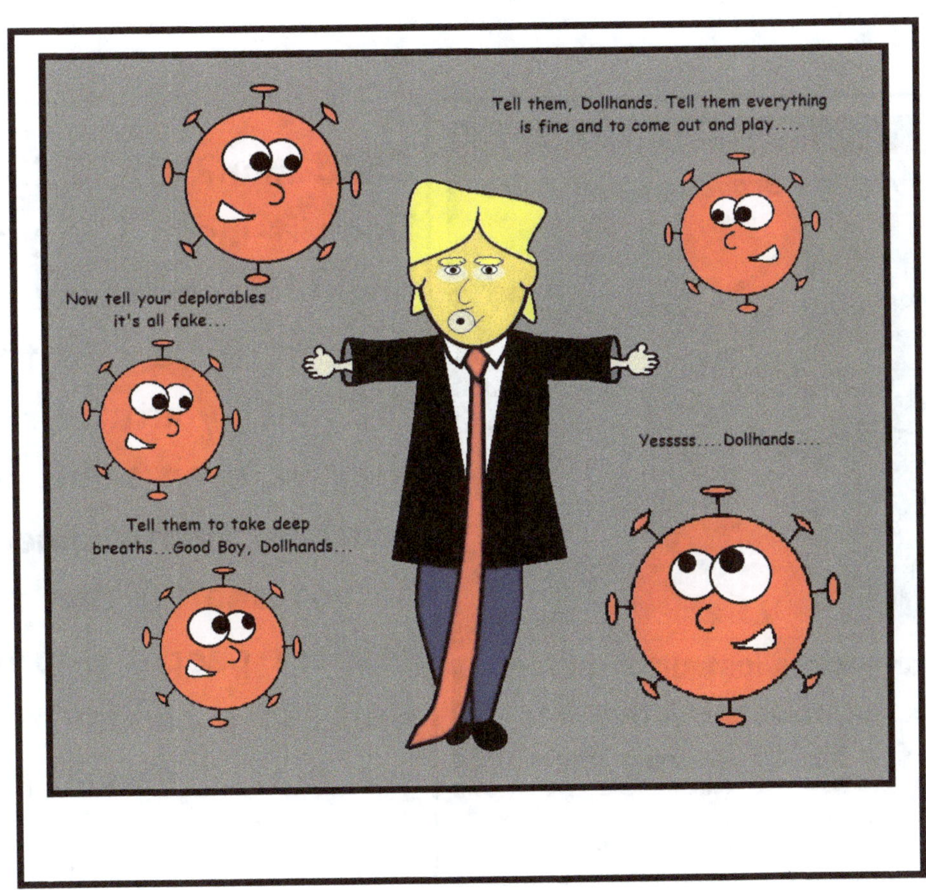

"Biden is promising to delay the vaccine and turn America into a prison state—locking you in your home while letting far-left rioters roam free. The Biden Lockdown will mean no school, no graduations, no weddings, no Thanksgiving, no Christmas, no Fourth of July!" - Dollhands

Child man? Oh, I like that. Does it mean I'm young at heart? I am! Many many experts have said that I'm the most youthful President they've ever seen. More youthful than Kennedy. And he got shot! I don't really respect people who get shot. It's harder to not get shot. I should know!

November 3rd, 2021

Dollhands T. Rump loses to the smart kid by over 7 MILLION VOTES

SEVEN

MILLION

VOTES!

November 9, 2020

"If Joe Biden were President, you wouldn't have the Vaccine for another four years, nor would the @US_FDA have ever approved it so quickly. The bureaucracy would have destroyed millions of lives" – sore loser

November 10, 2020

U.S. death toll passes 240,000

What I found most disturbing was how little he mentioned the virus after he lost the election. It was killing thousands of Americans and he would only whine once in a while, but it was obvious he cared more about losing an election than helping the American people. I guess he forgot he was still President. It wasn't suprising, not one bit, his entire life has been only about himself, but it was still disappointing to find out he still was unable to rise to the office. Sad little man.

November 18, 2020

U.S. death toll passes 250,000

November 19, 2020

Last Coronavirus Task Force press briefing under the Trump Administration.

November 24, 2020

U.S. death toll passes 260,000

December 7, 2020

U.S. death toll passes 280,000

December 8, 2020

Dollhands holds numerous White House holiday parties despite guidance from the CDC to limit indoor gatherings and curtail travel amid the spike in virus infections. Masks are not required, according to guests.

December 14, 2020

U.S. death toll passes 300,000

December 30, 2020

The Dollhands administration said 20 million COVID-19 vaccinations by the year's end. Only 2 million people have been vaccinated so far. Dollhands accomplished 'Warp Speed' about as well as he accomplished 'monogamy' with each of his wives.

January 3, 2021

Dollhands spends a day crying on Twitter. Poor dear.

"Something how Dr. Fauci is revered by the LameStream Media as such a great professional, having done, they say, such an incredible job, yet he works for me and the Dollhands Administration, and I am in no way given any credit for my work. Gee, could this just be more Fake News?"

"The number of cases and deaths of the China Virus is far exaggerated in the United States because of @CDCgov's ridiculous method of determination compared to other countries, many of whom report, purposely, very inaccurately and low. "When in doubt, call it Covid." Fake News!"

"The vaccines are being delivered to the states by the Federal Government far faster than they can be administered!"

January 6, 2021

Dollhands T. Rump, traitor to his own country, tells mob to attack Congress because he's sore-ass loser dipshit.

January 9, 2021

U.S. death toll passes 370,000

January 12, 2021

White House announces they will begin releasing vaccine doses that had been held in reserve for second shots, but no such reserve existed. Their false announcement raised false hopes among state and local officials.

January 13, 2021

U.S. death toll passes 380,000

January 20, 2021

Dollhand's last day in office sees over 400,000 American deaths from Covid

A Final Word From Dollhands T. Rump

(written by a ghost writer who knows actual words)

Congratulations! Not only did you get to see beautiful pictures of yours truly, and read some of my amazing observations, but your purchase of this book has helped pay for my legal fees…er ….re-election campaign to keep making America great!

First I would like to thank President Nixon, who turned a non-issue, abortion, into something that Evangelicals decided was so important they would overlook everything else the Republican Party does, just to save the unborn. Even though the Bible actually says "The stranger who resides with you shall be to you as one of your citizens; you shall love him as yourself, for you were strangers in the land of Egypt"….they let us build WALLS! It's hilarious. Even though that Jesus guy talked about caring for the poor, the sick and how important the children are, they let us screw with food stamps, take away child tax credits, try to destroy affordable healthcare and ignore the fact that kids are being shot, in school, on a weekly basis…all because we tell them it's Socialism and it has something to do with their guns being taken away. But man, bring up abortion and they're marching in the streets, even though the Bible doesn't mention it one time. Plus we get them to vote against Education, Healthcare and Alleviating Poverty, the three things EVERYONE knows is what actually lower abortions. They're literally causing more abortions by voting for Republicans, but we're not going to tell them, we like the power!

It's so funny!

Next I'd like to thank Sarah chick from Alaska. The Republican Party, before her, was just a bunch of conservative nerds who liked to deny that our deficit rose highest under Republican Presidents, a bunch of 'moral majority/family value' types who tried real hard to pretend the Republican Party wasn't full of misogynists, wife cheaters, pedophiles and the blatantly racists, who have had to keep their racism on the down low for many years, until they were finally able to share their thoughts when we had our first Black President. She was able to unite them all under the *Tea Party* label, give the dumbest and least informed a voice, and then let them start to scare actual lawmakers into doing things that would have been seen as treason during any other time in history.

I would also like to thank the Republican Party. Never has a Party been so willing to have POWER that they are willing to elect a three time wife cheater, pussy grabbing, racists, ignorant moron just because they knew it would appeal to the Deplorables in America, a group that makes up a majority of their base. They pretended to be offended when I first ran for office, but once they saw that my whipping up and exciting the inbred, the white supremacists and the morally bankrupt could gain them more power, they threw all their doubts aside and couldn't put on my red hat fast enough. Good for you realizing Power is more important than Integrity or the Constitution!

Lastly, I would like to thank the person that has made my rise to Glory possible....Satan. You told me all those years ago that if I just listened to you, and used fear and hate as my guiding principles, and preyed upon the weak, the ignorant and the vulnerable, that I could command a great army that would spread your lies under the guise of patriotism and Christianity. I doubted you when you said we could get almost half of this "Christian Nation" to support treating immigrants like shit, voting against healthcare that is saving actual lives, making it okay for children to be murdered in school on a weekly basis, overlooking my cheating on three wives, bragging about sexual assault, paying off porn stars, calling soldiers 'stupid', degrading a POW American Hero and saying things like Back the Blue and Blue Lives Matter, all while watching our very own people beat cops as they try to overturn a fair election...you said it was possible...and I apologize for doubting you. And the 'mark of the beast' being a red hat with MAGA on it that was *Made in China*...THAT was a stroke of genius! You are a true businessman! So thank you, dark lord, I hope I did you proud. And thank you for letting me borrow your daughter as a wife. She was cruel, but fascinating.

MAGA! – D.T.R.

If you enjoyed this book, cool, tell a friend!

If this book offended you, that's fine, you offend real Americans.